Visualizations for an Easier Childbirth

Carl Jones

Distributed by Simon & Schuster
New York, New York

Library of Congress Cataloging-in-Publication Data

Jones, Carl.
Visualizations for an easier childbirth/Carl Jones.
p. cm.
Bibliography: p.
1. Natural childbirth. 2. Visualization. 3. Imagery (Psychology) 4. Relaxation.
I. Title.
RG661.J59 1988 88-11951 618.4'5—dc19

ISBN 0-88166-119-8

Edited by Maureen Lucier

Published by Meadowbrook Press, 18318 Minnetonka Boulevard,
Deephaven, MN 55391

Cover Design: Marcie St. Clair

Cover Illustrator: Anastasia Mitchell

BOOK TRADE DISTRIBUTION by Simon & Schuster, a division of
Simon & Schuster, Inc., 1230 Avenue of the Americas, New York, NY 10020

S&S Ordering #: 0-671-67086-7

89 90 91 10 9 8 7 6 5 4 3 2

Printed in the United States of America

To Carl, Paul, and Jonathan,

with love.

Acknowledgments

Special thanks to the many, many parents who have shared with me the results of using visualization in labor. They have proven over and over again that this is, indeed, the most powerful method there is to reduce the fear and pain of childbirth and to help make birth the rewarding, fulfilling event every mother deserves.

Thanks to the innumerable childbirth educators, midwives, and physicians who have supported me with their enthusiasm about my work in what is, after all, a fresh approach to childbirth.

Thanks to the master craftsmen, Nate Martin and Ernie Johnson of Lancaster, New Hampshire, who, with their patience, unexcelled skill in woodworking, and always good humor in the face of my endless, exacting demands, managed to build the library that is now home to my collection of childbirth literature.

Thanks to Mimi and Fred Stiles and their thirteen-year-old son, Aaron, who, during the writing of this book, cared for our two older boys when our youngest had to be rushed to the hospital with a sudden illness.

And thanks, too, to my wife, Jan. Caring for our three boys (Carl, 7, Paul, 5, and Jonathan, 2) and working with an eccentric author is no easy business for even the most marvelous of women. Yet she always manages to type the manuscripts and meet the deadlines which, without her, I would invariably miss.

Contents

Introduction

Birth with
Less Stress

Virtually every pregnant woman has the same goal: a safe, happy birth for herself and her child.

The message of this book is that you *can* create the birth you truly desire. The method presented here—deep relaxation and creative visualization—opens the door to the most powerful resource you have for creating the birth you want: your inner self.

Anyone can use creative visualization. You can use it whether you plan to give birth at home, in a childbearing center, or in a hospital. Anyone planning to help a woman through labor will also find it effective. Even if you know nothing about childbirth, you can reduce the laboring mother's fear and pain by guiding her through the visualization exercises in this book.

Creative visualization is wonderfully flexible. You can combine it with any form of childbirth preparation, including breathing patterns. However, chances are that when you learn to use visualization you'll find breathing patterns practically unnecessary.

Chapter One

The Power of Creative Visualization

Creative visualization, sometimes called "creative imagery," is a method of translating positive thoughts into dynamic mental pictures or images to bring about a desired goal. This technique has enabled thousands to unlock the power of the mind in a wide variety of fields, from medicine to sports.

Since ancient times people have used creative visualization in magical ceremonies for healing. Today medicine taps the same power of the mind in a more scientific context. Deep relaxation and visualization are applied with hundreds of variations in holistic medicine (several branches of medicine that focus on the whole person: body, mind, and emotions). Biofeedback research has revealed startling information about the influence of visualization on the body. With deep relaxation and visualization, we can control bodily processes once believed to be entirely involuntary, such as heartbeat, blood pressure, and brain waves.

Dr. Herbert Benson of Beth Israel Hospital in Boston has found that simple meditation practiced regularly, can decrease blood pressure, oxygen consumption, and respiration rate, as well as bring about other significant physiologic changes. He has termed this the "relaxation response," the very opposite of the "flight or fight" response. According to Dr. Benson, learning to elicit the relaxation response may have a major role in treating diseases such as hypertension (high blood pressure).

In some forms of psychotherapy, creative visualization has played an integral role for decades. Among the many uses of visualization in this field are: reducing tension, facilitating problem solving, stimulating the imagination, realizing goals, and increasing control over one's inner and outer life.

In sports, this mind-over-body approach has sparked the enthusiasm of innumerable athletes who have discovered how mind/body relaxation combined with creative visualization can improve achievement. Visualizing the goals—an improved game—can actually help the athlete prepare for the game and heighten performance. For example, players at the Tennis Club in Boston are taught to relax while learning and then to visualize an ideal stroke to imprint the concept in their mind. According to Geoffrey C. Harvey, a teaching tennis pro, the purpose of this is to get the left hemisphere of the brain (the logical, rational part of the mind) out of the way and let the body "do its own thing" (Benson, 138). By mentally rehearsing a stroke, a shot, or an aspect of the game he wants to master, the athlete programs the mind to improve performance. Hundreds of athletes have discovered that the method works—often as well as physical practice!

This fascinating method of turning inward has become increasingly popular in stress management, development of business skills, child development, and education as well. But in no field is creative visualization more effective than in preparation for childbirth.

Benefits of Creative Visualization During Pregnancy and Childbirth

The visualization exercises in this book will enhance your childbearing experience in the following ways:

- help you relax
- reduce the fear of childbirth
- create or strengthen a positive view of birth
- heighten your intuition
- make you more aware of your baby's needs
- enhance prenatal bonding
- help you plan wisely for the birth
- reduce labor's pain
- increase the likelihood of a shorter labor
- lessen the chance of lacerations during birth
- reduce the likelihood of complications, including a cesarean section
- help you prepare for a smoother transition to parenthood
- reduce the likelihood of postpartum blues.

Of course, in addition to doing the visualization exercises, you will want to carefully choose a birthing place and a caregiver. See Chapter 2 for a discussion of how creative visualization can help you with these important choices.

What Parents and Experts Say About Creative Visualization

Lyla, a thirty-nine-year-old first-time mother, was very frightened of her labor until she discovered the power of creative visualization. "I doubted that I would be able to go through with it," she recalls. "But using creative visualization made me see that I had what it takes inside me to get rid of my fears and go through labor with a positive attitude." Though her labor was difficult at times, Lyla enjoyed a totally natural birth with no medication.

Creative visualization also helped Lyla's husband prepare for birth. "Peter was always afraid something would go wrong, that he wouldn't be able to help me. After doing visualization, he felt he could handle labor and support me even if something did happen."

Thousands of women have similar stories. Creative visualization has helped them through labor with less fear, less pain, and in less time.

Health professionals across the country who have used creative visualization in childbirth have likewise discovered that the method is amazingly effective.

"Mental visualization is the most powerful tool a couple can use to reduce the fear and pain of labor," says Suzanna May Hilbers, registered physical therapist and teacher trainer for ASPO/Lamaze, the world's largest childbirth education organization. She has taught the method to thousands of childbirth professionals and expectant parents. She emphasizes that with creative visualization, you give your mind a clear picture of what you want to achieve—a safe, rewarding birth. And by doing so, she says, you can actually "alter labor's physiology."

Dr. Emmett Miller, one of the nation's leading experts on relaxation and visualization, has used the method with laboring women for eighteen years. According to him, "Visualization can bring about deep relaxation, lead to a less physically traumatic birth and more pain-free delivery, and to less need for instrumental delivery and the use of anesthetic agents."

As many have discovered, the method can also reduce the chance of a cesarean section. Pat Jones, certified nurse-midwife in Houston, teaches her clients to relax deeply and visualize themselves enjoying a normal birth, "feeling the baby sliding out between your legs." This has helped scores of her clients birth naturally without surgery. "Though there are no studies to prove it yet," she says, "judging from my own practice, there is no question that this method lessens the chance of surgical birth."

Why Creative Visualization Works

Creative visualization is ideally suited to pregnancy

4

and labor. This is largely because labor is a *mind/body* process. Conditioning the mind for a relaxed and peaceful birth also prepares the body. Additionally, during pregnancy and labor you are particularly open to the power of visualization because of your increased right-brain orientation.

The Mind/Body Process of Labor

Labor is physiologically a sexual function. Though labor (associated with discomfort) and lovemaking (associated with pleasure) may seem poles apart, there are actually striking similarities between the two. Both take place in the sexual organs and involve the same hormone, oxytocin. Both respond to the woman's emotions. Both can be impaired by emotional conflicts and disturbances in the environment. And both work optimally when the woman embraces the experience with a positive attitude.

Everyone is aware of the effects of emotion—mood, setting, love—on satisfying lovemaking. The mind's influence on labor is just as dramatic. Though it is an involuntary function, labor is highly sensitive to the mother's thoughts and feelings, her environment, and the attitudes of those around her, particularly her caregiver. Whatever affects the laboring mother's mind affects her body. If she is tense or overly anxious, in an unsupportive environment, or has a deep emotional conflict about childbirth or becoming a parent, her labor is bound to be affected.

There is nothing mystical about the relationship of the mind to labor. You can easily understand how fear, for example, increases the pain and the length of labor. A contraction begins. The mother becomes afraid. She tenses. Tension causes the muscles around the cervix to tighten. Longer and harder contractions are therefore necessary to open the tight cervix. Tension also decreases the available oxygen to the uterus, leading to more painful contractions. The pain triggers more fear which in turn causes greater tension, and so the cycle spirals.

Dr. Grantly Dick-Read, obstetrician and pioneer in natural childbirth, called this the "fear-tension-pain" cycle. Creative visualization can break this cycle by reducing fear and eliminating unnecessary tension.

Emotions also influence labor on a less easily ob-served level. For instance, negative feelings can inhibit the hor-monal balance necessary for laboring efficiently just as they can inhibit sexual response. The hormone oxytocin, released by the anterior pituitary gland to help regulate uterine contractions, is, according to Dr. Niles Newton, professor of behavioral science at Northwestern University Medical School, "easily conditioned and inhibited by outside stimuli." Oxytocin is less likely to be released if the mother is very upset. At the same time, stress hormones released when she is tense can impair labor.

By making you feel more secure and comfortable during labor, visualization assists you to achieve the optimal hormonal balance to labor efficiently.

Creative visualization helps to bring about a state of complete mind/body relaxation—the major key to reducing the pain and length of labor. Relaxation and creative visualization work hand in hand to help you surrender to the miraculous process that brings your child into the world. By surrendering to labor, you flow with, rather than fight against, your contractions.

Increased Right-Brain Orientation

Another reason creative visualization is so successful for labor can be partly explained in terms of the hemispheres of the brain. Visualization utilizes the intuitive, creative side of the brain—the *right hemisphere*, sometimes called the "heart brain." Rational thinking and logic, on the other hand, are associated with the *left hemisphere*.

During pregnancy the *right* hemisphere seems to become more dominant—the mother becomes more intuitive and more focused inward. The right hemisphere also dominates during labor. As a result of your increased right hemisphere orientation during pregnancy and labor, you are especially open to creative visualization. In fact, during pregnancy and labor you are probably more open to the power of creative visualization than at any other time in your life.

How Creative Visualization Prepares You for Childbirth

With visualization you present your inner mind with a clear picture of your goal—flowing smoothly with contractions and enjoying a safe, happy birth. Janet Tipton, a midwife practicing in eastern Texas who has used this method with scores of clients, compares it with "the technique athletes use to program themselves for peak perfomances." By visualizing yourself handling contractions peacefully, you "program" yourself for a peaceful birth experience. After doing this repeatedly, you come to believe in your goal as an accomplished reality. This orients you physically, psychologically, and emotionally toward achieving what you have imagined. It mobilizes all your resources to create the birth you want.

- *Creative visualization develops a positive attitude toward childbirth.* This does not mean that you deny the reality of hard work and pain. However, it does mean letting go of negative images about birth, such as the notion that childbirth is dangerous or a medical crisis, and accepting birth as a natural, normal event. If you have positive feelings about birth, you are more likely to have a positive birth experience. You will find it easier to let go and let your body "do its own thing," thereby laboring more efficiently.

- *Creative visualization develops confidence in your ability to give birth normally.* This goes hand in hand with developing a positive view of birth. When you view birth as the normal and natural event that it is—part of the mother's sexuality—you become more secure in your ability to give birth in harmony with nature. In addition, as you repeatedly picture yourself going through labor with a minimum of stress, you begin to realize that you really *can* cope with childbirth successfully. When you approach labor with confidence rather than self-doubt, most likely you will automatically do whatever best helps your labor to progress—such as choosing the optimal labor and birthing positions.

7

- *Visualization provides a means of self-direction.* As you practice the exercises in this book, you may begin to think of practical ways to make what you imagine a reality. You may have flashes of insight about certain aspects of your diet, your birth plans, your baby's care—or any number of things that can contribute to a safe, more rewarding birth.
- *Creative visualization inspires self-reflection.* You may become more aware of and begin to examine your feelings about childbirth. This gives you an opportunity to recognize and replace negative views with positive ones, helping you release emotional blocks that might otherwise interfere with normal labor.

For example, one woman dreaded labor. During her sessions of relaxation and visualization, she discovered that she was not emotionally ready to become a mother. She was afraid she couldn't handle the responsibility. When she faced this feeling and discussed it with her mate, she began to make preparations for her new role and to accept herself as a parent. Her fear of labor almost vanished, and she began to prepare for birth with confidence.

To sum up, regular use of the exercises in this book creates the ideal conditions for mind and body to work in harmony during labor. In effect, using creative visualization links you with your instinctive self. It puts you in touch with the part of you that already knows how to give birth perfectly.

Chapter Two

How to Use Creative Visualization

Using creative visualization is easy and enjoyable. Anyone can learn this simple method to enjoy a more fulfilling pregnancy and help prepare for a safe, rewarding birth.

General Guidelines

The following guidelines apply to all the visualization exercises in this book:

- Practice visualization regularly—a few minutes each day, two or three days a week, or more often if you prefer.

- Practice visualization in any comfortable position—sitting cross-legged on the floor, sitting in a chair, semi-reclining, lying down—as long as you are completely relaxed.

- Do visualization exercises in a quiet, dimly lit, or dark room. Set aside a time when you will not be disturbed. Take the phone off the hook. Put your responsibilities aside. Don't think about what you have to do next, problems you need to solve, tasks that should be accomplished. This is your time to relax and enjoy yourself.

- Practice when your mind and body are relaxed. Creative visualization works most effectively at this time. To achieve complete relaxation, use one of the exercises in Chapter 3, "Relaxing Mind and Body." Then, while deeply relaxed, go on with one of the visualization exercises in this book.

- Read through the visualization exercise before beginning and before relaxing mind and body. If it is a long exercise, don't try to commit every detail to memory. Don't worry if you miss something. You can always do the exercise again later.

- As you do the exercise, allow your mind to fill in as many details as you like. Involve all of your senses whenever possible—touch, smell, taste, sight, and hearing.

- Don't be concerned if you don't "visualize" distinct mental pictures. You may see a clear picture in your mind's eye, or you may simply "sense" an image.

- Use strong positive suggestions with your visualization, such as "I am becoming more and more relaxed," "I can labor in perfect harmony with nature," "I am fully able to cope with labor," and so forth. Positive suggestions, sometimes called "affirmations," empower the exercise. Using affirmations is further discussed in Chapter 4, "Inner Preparation for Childbirth."

- If you are interrupted at any time, or if your mind wanders, simply return to the point where you left off and continue with the exercise.

- Feel free to alter any of the exercises in this book to suit your own tastes. Change the words and the images themselves in any way that you wish. Not everyone responds in the same way to the same images.

- At the end of each exercise, gradually return to the world of everyday life. All the exercises in this book suggest: "Count slowly to five, stretch gently, and open your eyes." This provides a transition between the deeply relaxed state accompanying an visualization exercise and your normal waking consciousness.

- If you prefer, your mate or friend can read the directions to you as you do the exercise.

Instructions for Guiding Someone Through Visualization

1. Read through the exercise first.
2. Read the exercise aloud *slowly* in a soft voice.
3. Pause between each step to allow plenty of time to complete the step.

- Try using a cassette tape to guide you through the visualization exercise. You, your mate, or a friend can record the exercises, or you can purchase one of several tapes. (See "Recommended Reading.")

For your first visualization exercise, do The Special Place in Chapter 4. During this exercise you create your own peaceful inner sanctuary. The Special Place deepens your state of relaxation and provides an inner retreat to which you can mentally retire during labor or at any other time when you feel tense. Once you have done The Special Place, try Radiant Light. Then move on to the other visualization exercises.

Don't wait until labor begins to do the visualization exercises for labor in Chapter 6 (pages 56–63). Read through them now. Practice them a few times. Your mate, too, should become familiar with them. When you are in labor, he can guide you through whichever visualization exercises you prefer.

Creating Your Own Visualizations

Design your own images if you wish. No one knows better than you what images make you feel relaxed and confident.

If you create your own visualization exercises, keep the following points in mind:

- When planning a visualization exercise to help you achieve a specific goal, define the goal clearly in your mind. Choose a realistic goal that you truly desire and that you believe you can achieve.

- Always picture the goal as *having already been accomplished.* This presents the goal to your inner mind as a reality rather than a mere wish.

- Choose images that make you feel relaxed, comfortable, and confident. Experiment until you find the images you like best.

- Choose images that *feel right* for you. An image that makes one person feel comfortable may not have the same pleasant connotations for another. For example, you might find images of lying on a warm sandy beach very relaxing, while someone else might associate this image with sunburn and sandflies.

- Bear in mind that visualization often works in metaphor. A good example is *The Blossoming Flower* in Chapter 6. In this exercise, the flower symbolizes the cervix and/or vagina opening gradually and gracefully. Don't worry about whether or not the metaphor you choose precisely resembles the object or situation you wish to depict. If the metaphor has meaning for you, your subconscious mind will make the connection.

- Accompany your visualization exercises with affirmations whenever possible. These strong positive statements are the most effective when combined with visualization. See Chapter 4 for more about affirmations.

● End your visualization exercises with an expression of gratitude and inner fulfillment. This presents the goal as an already accomplished reality to your inner mind.

● Repeat your visualization often.

Creating the Birth You Want

Creative visualization can assist you to achieve a safe, happy birth. To make this method work most effectively, however, your intuition and logic must work in harmony.

Pay attention to your intuition. As mentioned in Chapter 1, one way visualization helps create a safe, fulfilling birth is by providing *self-direction*. Visualization can inspire you to think of ideas to help make your goal a reality. It is important to follow through on these ideas when appropriate.

Suppose, for example, that you visualize yourself having a natural, unmedicated birth in a peaceful surroundings. Meanwhile, you are planning to give birth in a hospital with a high cesarean rate and your present physician has a reputation for using an episiotomy with every birth. Clearly, to improve your chance of achieving your goal, you must make changes in your birth plans, such as choosing another hospital or physician. In this way, you combine visualization with concrete action to help achieve the birth you want.

The following sections discuss practical concerns you will need to consider in planning your baby's birth. Creative visualization can help you get in touch with your feelings on an intuitive basis for analyzing options.

Childbirth Goals

Clearly formulate your birth goal. A goal clearly defined is a goal half attained. Say, for example, that you want to birth naturally. Try to be as specific as possible about what this means to you. Does it mean birth at home? Birth without medical intervention? Birth without drugs? Breastfeeding without interruption immediately after the baby is born? If you are able to clearly define your goal, your inner mind will be better able to help you achieve it.

Childbirth Education

Learn as much as you can about childbirth by reading and by attending classes. For a complete discussion of the mind/body approach to childbirth, see the book *Mind over Labor*.

If you take childbirth classes, choose a childbirth educator who shares your philosophy of birth. The best classes are small—not more than ten couples. As a general rule, good childbirth classes take place in private homes or on other neutral ground. Many classes taught in hospitals are excellent; however, some reflect the institution's policies and are more concerned about creating compliant patients than informing you of your options and helping you achieve your individual goals.

Carolyn, a new mother, recalls: "In our class the instructor showed us films of mothers surrounded by medical machinery and husbands dressed in surgical gowns—as if this was the way birth had to be! But this wasn't how my husband and I planned to have our baby." As this example suggests, choosing another class or educating yourself at home, if necessary, is far preferable to attending a class that does not meet your needs.

Birth Plans

Take responsibility for your birth experience. This is a major step toward making it fulfilling. Your experience is shaped by the plans you make during pregnancy, so make plans conducive to your goal. Poor birth plans can undo all the benefits you gain with creative visualization.

Choose your caregiver and birthing environment carefully. This can spell the difference between a rewarding birth and a disappointing, frustrating experience. Make these important choices with your mate. Both of you should feel comfortable with them.

Choice of Caregiver

Choose a physician or midwife who fully supports your goals. There are radical differences in the way caregivers practice. Some actively manage labor throughout, with intravenous feeding, routine electronic monitoring, episiotomy (surgical incision to enlarge the birth outlet as the baby is being born), and other medical procedures. Other caregivers view birth as a natural event and intervene only if absolutely necessary.

Bear in mind that when you hire a caregiver to give prenatal care and attend your birth, you are inviting this person to share one of your most intimate life events. Be sure it is someone with whom you feel compatible.

Enlist the aid of your inner mind. The visualization exercises *Inner Voice Imagery* (pages 34–35), *The Journey* (pages 35–36), and *The Invitation* (pages 40–41) in Chapter 4 can help you make or evaluate your choice of caregiver.

Choice of Birthing Environment

The birthing environment has a profound effect on your labor. As discussed in Chapter 1, labor—like lovemaking—is a mind/body process. Your emotions influence labor's physiology. Laboring in an environment where you are uncomfortable and anxious can contribute to a longer labor, fetal distress, and a traumatic birth for you and your child. A wise choice of birthing environment, on the other hand, contributes to a shorter, less uncomfortable labor and decreases the likelihood of complications, including cesarean birth.

Knowing that you and your baby are safe—that expert care is available should it be needed—is of the greatest importance. Your physical and emotional comfort, however, are also essential. Choose a setting where you feel emotionally supported.

Wherever you give birth, you and your mate should feel that you are in charge. You should be free to behave the way you wish during labor without inhibition, to birth in whatever position you choose, to interact spontaneously with your partner, and to invite whomever you wish to share your birth.

Visit the birthing place with your mate *before* making a final choice.

Use visualization to help you make your decision. The exercises *Inner Voice Imagery* (pages 34–35), *The Journey* (pages 35–36), and *Birthplace* (pages 41–42) in Chapter 4 and the exercise *Talking with Your Baby* (pages 49–50) in Chapter 5 can help you choose or evaluate your birthing place.

If you plan to give birth in a hospital or childbearing center, become familiar with the birthing place before labor. This will lessen your anxiety, enable you to better flow with your labor, and lessen your mate's inhibitions about giving labor support. One way to feel more at home in your birthing place is to incorporate the setting into visualization exercises. You can easily imagine yourself in your chosen birthing place when you do the exercise *Birthplace* (pages 41–42) in Chapter 4.

Explore your feelings and attitudes about childbirth through visualization. While deeply relaxed you may begin to let your feelings come to the surface. Reflect on your feelings and let them guide you in formulating your childbirth goals.

Remain *flexible* and *open-minded*. As you learn more about childbirth, you may redesign your goals or think of new goals altogether. You may also want to make changes in your birth plans to enable you to enjoy the safe, rewarding, wonderful birth experience that you imagine.

Chapter Three

Relaxing
Mind
and Body

Mastering relaxation is essential both to decrease labor's discomfort and to use creative visualization efficiently.

If you are able to greet labor with relaxation, you are able to cooperate with, rather than fight the process that brings your baby into the world. You become a partner, not an adversary, of the life-creating force.

During labor, powerful contractions massage your baby, preparing him for his first breath. At the same time, the contractions open a gateway for your baby to pass from the womb to your waiting arms. The amazingly stretchable cervix and vagina open like a blossoming flower. This soft tissue most readily yields to your baby if you are able to relax. The likelihood of lacerations is also decreased when you are relaxed.

Tension, on the other hand, causes the cervix to remain tight, resistant to opening. This means that contractions may have to last longer to overcome the resistance. Relaxation, therefore, is the key to a shorter, more comfortable labor.

Relaxation is also important to make efficient use of visualization. When you are wholly relaxed, your mind is more open to positive suggestion *and* you can more readily tap your inner resources. To make your visualization most effective and enjoyable, first relax totally by doing one of the relaxation exercises in this chapter. Then use one of the creative visualization exercises that appear later in this book. You will probably find that the more you practice, the easier it will be to relax.

Guidelines for Relaxation Exercises

- Practice relaxation as often as you can—that may be every day, or only two or three times a week.

- Practice relaxation in a quiet, dimly lit room.

- Wear loose, comfortable clothing. Remove your shoes. If you wear glasses, remove them.

- Practice relaxation and visualization in any comfortable position, sitting or lying down. Two comfortable positions are:

  Back-lying (supine) position with hands at your sides. When first learning the art of deep relaxation, many find this position best. However, you should *avoid lying flat on your back if it makes you uncomfortable in any way.* During late pregnancy the supine position causes the weight of the uterus to depress vessels in the circulatory system, inhibiting the return of blood from the lower part of the body. This can lead to feeling faint and dizzy and to numbness in the legs, and can result in less oxygen for the baby. Symptoms are immediately relieved with a change of position.

  Side-lying with your head and shoulder supported by pillows and a pillow between your legs if desired.

- First read through the directions and then do the exercise. Or your partner or a friend can read the directions to you in a soft voice as you follow them. The person reading the directions should pause between each step, giving you plenty of time to complete that step before going on.

● You can also use audio cassette tapes with prerecorded relaxation instructions. Many find this a very effective way to bring about a deep state of mind/body relaxation. One of the finest cassettes available is Dr. Emmett Miller's *Letting Go of Stress*, which includes the exercises *Progressive Relaxation* and *Autogenic Stress Release*.

Relaxation Exercises

These exercises can be used at any time during pregancy—alone or as preliminaries to creative visualization exercises.

Progressive Relaxation

This exercise, which owes its name to the book *Progressive Relaxation* by Edmund Jacobson, is a very effective way to let go of stress and teach your body the feeling of total relaxation.

Step by step you tense and relax one group of muscles at a time until you have achieved deep relaxation. It takes quite a while the first few times you try it. With experience, however, you will probably find that you can release muscular tension in much less time.

Get into a comfortable position.

Close your eyes.

Breathe deeply and rhythmically.

The abdomen should rise on the in-breath and fall on the out-breath.

Breathe this way for a minute or so, putting aside all responsibilities.

Now, tighten the muscles of your left arm and hand, making a fist. Hold for a few seconds.

Release, letting your arm and hand relax.

Feel the relaxation in your arm and hand.

Tighten the muscles of your right arm and hand, clenching your fist. Hold for a few seconds.

Release, letting your arm and hand relax.

Feel the relaxation in your arm and hand.

As you continue this exercise, take a few seconds to feel the relaxation each time you release a muscle group.

Tighten the muscles of your left leg and foot, curling your toes.

Release, letting your leg and foot relax.

Tighten the muscles of your right leg and foot, curling the toes.

Release, letting your leg and foot relax.

Squeeze your buttocks together.

Release, letting your buttocks relax.

Tighten the muscles of the pelvic floor as if you are trying to keep from urinating.

Release, feeling the muscles of the pelvic floor relax.

Arch your back slightly.

Release, letting the muscles of your back relax.

Tighten your shoulders by pushing them back as if you are trying to make your shoulder blades touch one another.

Release, letting your shoulders relax.

Tighten the muscles of your neck by arching your neck slightly as if you are trying to look up.

Release, letting your neck relax.

Clench your teeth together, tightening the muscles of your jaw.

Release, feeling the muscles in your jaw relax.

Squint your eyes.

Release, letting your eyelids relax.

Furrow your brow.

Release, letting the space between your eyes feel as if it is getting wider.

Now take a few deep breaths.

As you do so, let your breathing become a little slower, a little deeper, without forcing the breath in any way.

Feel any additional tension melting away as you exhale. Each breath out makes you feel more and more relaxed.

Now let your awareness travel throughout your body.

If you find any areas that could be more relaxed, feel the tension melt away as you breathe out.

Enjoy the feeling of complete relaxation for a few minutes.

Then, when you are ready, gently stretch, and open your eyes.

Or, remain in your relaxed state with eyes closed and go on with one of the visualization imagery exercises in this book.

Autogenic Stress Release

This very pleasant and effective exercise brings about a state of deep relaxation through the use of rhythmic breathing and suggestion. It is based on autogenic therapy, a method of mind/body relaxation and healing developed in the 1920s by Dr. J. H. Schultz.

Get into a comfortable position.

Close your eyes.

Inhale deeply and slowly through the nose. Exhale through slightly parted lips.

Continue to breathe this way for a minute or so.

Now, let your breathing become a little deeper, a little slower, without forcing the breath in any way.

Continue to breathe in this slow, relaxing way throughout the exercise.

Now, with each breath in and each breath out, mentally repeat the following words: My right arm is warm and relaxed.

After a couple of deep breaths, turn your attention to your left arm.

With each breath in and each breath out, mentally say: My left arm is warm and relaxed.

Now, with each breath in and each breath out, say: My right leg is warm and relaxed.

Now, with each breath in and each breath out, say: My left leg is warm and relaxed.

Now say: My uterus and pelvic organs are warm and relaxed.

Observe your breathing, calm and regular.

With the next breath out, say: My breathing is effortless.

Now say: The muscles of my back and neck are warm and relaxed.

After a half minute or so, with the next breath out say: My jaw muscles are loose and relaxed.

Now, with the next breath out say: My forehead is cool and relaxed.

With the next breath out say: My eyelids are heavy and relaxed.

Enjoy the sensation of complete relaxation for a minute or so.

Tell yourself: Because I can relax, I can labor and give birth better.

When you are ready, take a deep breath, stretch gently, and open your eyes.

Or, remain in your relaxed state with eyes closed and go on with one of the visualization exercises in this book.

Circulating the Life Breath

This exercise, adapted from *Mind Over Labor*, combines rhythmic breathing with mental imagery to leave you feeling deeply relaxed and revitalized. You imagine that with each breath you take in you are drawing in a vital life force and circulating it throughout your body as you become more and more relaxed.

Get into a comfortable position.

Close your eyes.

Breathe deeply and rhythmically.

Let your breathing become a little deeper, a little slower, without forcing the breath in any way.

Breathe this way for a minute or so.

Now, as you inhale, imagine that your breath is a radiant golden light, filling your body.

Exhale, feeling your body relax.

Inhale and imagine that the golden energy of your breath is filling your left arm and hand.

Exhale, feeling the tension flowing away through your fingertips.

Inhale and imagine that your breath is filling your right arm and hand.

Exhale, feeling the tension draining away through your fingertips.

Inhale and imagine that the radiant golden light is filling your left leg and foot.

Exhale, feeling the tension flowing away through the sole of your foot.

Inhale and imagine that the radiant light is filling your right leg and foot.

Exhale, feeling the tension flowing away through the sole of your foot.

Inhale and imagine that the radiant energy is filling your pelvic region, the buttocks, and the birth canal.

Exhale, as if you were breathing out through the birth canal, feeling all the tension flowing away.

Inhale and imagine the radiant light filling your abdominal region.

Exhale, feeling the tension flowing away from the abdominal area.

Inhale and imagine the radiant light flowing down the spine, filling the chest and back with energy.

Exhale, feeling the tension flowing away as your chest and back relax.

Inhale and imagine the radiant light filling your head and neck with life-giving energy.

Exhale, feeling all tension flowing away from your head and neck.

Now imagine that your breath is sweeping over you with a gentle wave of radiant light. Imagine that the light flows from the top of your head to the soles of your feet.

As your breath continues to sweep over you, let yourself go into a more relaxed state.

Enjoy the feeling of being totally relaxed for a few

minutes.

Then, when you are ready, take a deep breath, gently stretch, and open your eyes.

Or, remain in your relaxed state with eyes closed and go on with one of the visualization exercises in this book.

Chapter Four

Inner Preparation for Childbirth

What happens during pregnancy is nothing less than awesome. You are performing a miracle. Your body has made a new being. You and your baby are undergoing changes that are so rapid and so complex they stagger the imagination. Every organ and every part of your body, from the surface of your skin to the blood flowing through your veins, is affected.

Creative visualization is probably more effective during these life-creating months than at any other time. This is largely because your thoughts turn inward as your baby grows and develops. You become more introspective. You are in closer touch with your inner mind. As stated in Chapter 1, you are oriented more to the right brain hemisphere, or "heart brain," during pregnancy. For this reason, you are especially open to positive suggestions and to the right hemisphere process of creative visualization.

Creative visualization offers many benefits during the prenatal months. When regularly used, visualization:

- promotes deep mind/body relaxation

- makes you feel healthier

- helps tap your inner resources and increases prenatal intuition

- puts you in closer touch with your creative energy

- develops confidence in your ability to give birth normally

- helps you make concrete decisions such as choosing a caregiver and birthing environment

- widens your perspective of birth

- helps you achieve your goal of a safe, rewarding birth.

Using mental visualization is easy. However, you must be willing to put in a little time and energy to make it work effectively.

Affirmations

An affirmation is a positive statement—often about a state of mind you wish to develop, such as more confidence, or a situation you would like to bring about. Repeated often, affirmations can help you overcome negative thought patterns and assist you to make your goals a reality.

The best time to use an affirmation is while in a state of deep mind/body relaxation when you are doing a visualization exercise. Your inner mind is most open to suggestion at these times. But you can use affirmations any time you choose. You may find it helpful to write a positive thought down on an index card and put the card on the bathroom mirror or in some other place where it can be read often.

Follow the guidelines below when you use affirmations:

- Feel free to change the wording of any of the positive suggestions in this book. Or, create your own affirmations to best meet your needs.

- Make your affirmations short, simple, and meaningful to you. Repeat them with feeling. The more energy and belief you put behind a statement, the more effective it will be.

- Phrase affirmations in the *present*, not the future. For example, say: "I am able to give birth naturally" rather than "I will be able to give birth naturally."

- Phrase affirmations in a positive way, such as, "I am able to give birth naturally" rather than "I will not have a cesarean section."

Don't think of affirmations as "Band-Aids" to mask negative feelings. It is important to acknowledge your feelings, both negative and positive. As Shakti Gawain points out in *Creative Visualization*, "Affirmations are not meant to *contradict* or *try to change* your feelings or emotions .... but affirmations can help you create a new point of view about life which will enable you to have more and more satisfying experiences from now on" (Gawain 39).

Affirmations for the Expectant Mother

Pregnancy is beautiful.

I enjoy the feeling of new life within me.

I am able to provide all that my baby needs to grow and be healthy.

Childbirth is a normal, healthy event.

I am creating a safe, healthy birth for myself and my baby.

My mate and I are the center of the childbearing experience.

I take responsibility to plan my birth wisely.

I choose a caregiver who respects my goals and helps me enjoy the birth I truly want.

I choose a childbirth environment that makes me feel secure and comfortable and that is a good place to begin a family.

I am able to flow with labor in perfect harmony with nature.

I am preparing my mind and my home for my child.

Affirmations for the Expectant Father

Pregnancy is beautiful.

Childbirth is a normal, healthy event.

My mate and I are the center of the childbearing experience.

My mate and I are working harmoniously toward a safe, rewarding birth.

I am learning everything I can to make birth a beautiful event for my family.

I make the best choices for a healthy, joyful birth.

I am able to reduce my partner's fear and pain with the support I provide during labor.

Visualization Exercises for Pregnancy

The following exercises can all be used at any time during pregnancy. Many can also be used during labor. Those which don't deal specifically with pregnancy and birth—The Special Place and The Radiant Light—can be used at other stressful times as well.

The Special Place

One of the most popular visualization exercises, The Special Place is an effective aid to deep relaxation during pregnancy, labor, or at any other time. During this exercise, you create your own private sanctuary—an inner environment of perfect peace, comfort, and security. Practice this visualization during pregnancy. When you are in labor, you will be able to imagine yourself in *The Special Place* to help you relax and feel comfortable and secure.

Relax completely, body and mind.

Put your responsibilities aside for a while.

For the next few minutes, there is nothing you need to do, no problem you need to solve.

This is your time to relax and be at peace.

Breathe deeply and rhythmically.

Let your breathing become a little deeper, a little slower, without forcing the breath in any way.

Now imagine that you are in a peaceful, special place, a place that makes you feel comfortable and totally secure.

It can be any place at all: real or imaginary, a mountain top, a valley by a bubbling brook, a moss-carpeted spot in a woodland grove, a meadow dotted with wildflowers, a room where you feel comfortable, whatever makes you feel perfectly secure.

Take a few minutes to let the details of this special place unfold before your mind's eye.

If distracting thoughts come into your mind, imagine that they are little puffs of white clouds carried away by the breeze on a clear spring day. And let them drift away.

Explore your special place. Enjoy being there.

Acknowledge that this is your own place. No one can enter without your invitation.

You can return to your special place anytime you want to feel peaceful and completely relaxed.

Spend as much time in your special place as you wish. When you are ready to return to your everyday life, count slowly to five, stretch gently, and open your eyes.

While creating your special place, use as many details as you want—sights, sounds, odors, impressions—to enjoy this visualization fully. Create the special place that feels just right for you. You may find images that convey warmth relaxing: a sandy beach, a couch by a fireplace in a cozy room. Or, you may prefer imagining a cool bed of moss by a bubbling brook.

Experiment until you find the special place that most appeals to you.

Once you have created a special place that feels just right, share the details of this place with your partner. If you wish, invite him to take an inner journey to this special place with you.

When you are in labor, he can help you relax, guiding you through the imagery of your peaceful inner sanctuary (see page 11 in Chapter 2 for intructions on how to guide someone through visualization exercises).

The Radiant Light

This peaceful exercise leaves you feeling relaxed, revitalized, and attuned to your creative energy.

Do it any time during pregnancy.

Relax completely, body and mind.

Focus your attention on your breathing, your breath flowing in and out.

Dwell just on your breathing for a minute or two. Follow your breath in and out without trying to control it. Each breath out melts tension away, leaving you more and more relaxed.

Enjoy the feeling of complete relaxation.

Now let your breathing become a little deeper, a little slower, without forcing the breath in any way.

Pause after every breath out and again after every breath in.

With each pause, tell yourself that you are entering a deeper, more relaxed state of body and mind.

Now imagine that your in-breath is a soft, radiant, golden light.

Imagine that you are breathing this golden light directly into your womb.

Imagine that the radiant light is filling your womb with health-giving energy.

As you continue to breathe this soft light in, imagine that it begins to radiate outward from your womb to fill your entire being.

Let yourself drift into even deeper relaxation, body and mind, as the radiant light fills your being.

Now imagine that the light is radiating out from you in all directions, a beautiful golden aura or halo.

If you wish, imagine the light is radiating out from you to surround your mate.

Let it radiate farther and farther from you until it fills your entire home.

Dwell on the image of the soft, radiant light filling your being and expanding in all directions around you for as long as you wish.

Then, when you are ready, slowly count to five and open your eyes.

Pregnant Body Beautiful

The pregnant woman has her own special beauty—a radiant beauty unlike any other. It's as if she were surrounded by a magnetic aura. Almost magically, she draws attention from all quarters. Even the glances of strangers linger on her.

This visualization centers on the miracle your body is working. It helps you feel more comfortable with your changing prenatal body and develop confidence in your ability to birth naturally.

Spend as long as you want at this exercise. Vary it any way you wish.

Relax completely, body and mind.

Begin with *The Radiant Light* visualization exercise (pages 31–32).

Now center your mind in your womb.

The womb is the source of all the changes that are taking place within your body, in your emotions, and even in your home right now.

Imagine that you are able to look within your womb.

Look at your baby: head down in a beautiful shimmering sac filled with crystal-clear fluid, in his or her own private universe.

Look at the beautiful curly bluish-white umbilical cord.

Follow the umbilical cord to the placenta attached to your uterine wall.

Imagine the oxygen and nutrients flowing from your body through the placenta, down the umbilical cord to your baby.

Tell yourself: I am able to supply all that my baby needs to grow and be healthy.

Consider what your body has done.

If you can do what you have done already, you can surely labor normally.

Tell yourself: I am able to labor in perfect harmony with nature.

Thank your body for the miracle it is working and will continue to work.

When you are ready, count slowly to five, stretch gently, and open your eyes.

Inner Voice Imagery

In most cases your body and your inner mind know just what you most need to enjoy a healthy, happy pregnancy and a safe, rewarding birth. This exercise puts you in touch with your inner feelings and needs. It can also help you be aware of and clear away any possible blocks preventing you from achieving your childbirth goals.

Relax completely, body and mind.

Begin with *The Special Place* exercise (pages 29–31).

Enjoy your special place for a few minutes. Then ask yourself *one* of the following questions:

• What do I most need to do to enjoy a healthy pregnancy?

• What do I most need to do to prepare for a safe, rewarding birth?

• What do I most need to do to prepare for the first weeks with my baby?

If thoughts or images come into your mind, let them drift freely. Just observe whatever thoughts or images arise.

Then, when you are ready, take a deep breath, count slowly to five, stretch gently, and open your eyes.

While doing Inner Voice Imagery, you may get a general impression of something you ought to do—develop confidence, improve your diet, exercise more, and so forth. Or you may receive a specific answer to your question. For example, in answer to the question "What do I most need to do right now to prepare for a safe, rewarding birth?" one expectant father had a strong feeling that he should learn more about labor support. "It was clear to me that I should acquire as much information as I could to reduce Joan's discomfort." He read a couple of books with his wife and learned things about reducing fear and pain that hadn't been taught in their childbirth class.

If you receive an answer, analyze it in the light of common sense. Does the answer make sense to you? If so, how can you apply it? For best results, intuition and logic should work hand in hand.

The Journey

In this exercise you take a mental journey anywhere you want and fantasize about your birth. Don't be concerned about being realistic. Let go. Be creative. Let your fantasy be exotic if you wish. Imagine yourself on a tropical island attended by midwives. Or laboring in the emerald green water of a beautiful sea. Or in a hospital or birthing center that has everything you could possibly want right at your fingertips. Or picture yourself in your own home.

The purpose of this visualization is to relax and enjoy yourself, to fantasize and explore new worlds. At the same time, this exercise helps you develop a fresh perspective of childbirth.

Relax completely, body and mind.

Put your responsibilities aside for a few minutes. You can return to them in a little while.

There is nowhere you need to go, nothing you need to do but this.

Imagine that you are on the shore of a river.

A boat drifts close to you.

You get on the boat.

The boat drifts gently along the river. It is taking you somewhere you really want to be.

Hear the sound of the water gently lapping the sides of the boat. Feel the warm sunlight.

Feel the cool breeze. Smell the fresh, fragrant air.

Enjoy the journey for a while.

After a few minutes, the boat comes to another shore.

You get off the boat and explore.

Now imagine that this is the place where you are giving birth.

See yourself in labor attended by whomever you want.

Let the scene unfold before your mind's eye. Take your time about this. Fill in as many details as you want—sights, sounds, odors, whatever you wish.

If there is something about the scene that you do not like, change it.

Enjoy this birthing scene for as long as you wish.

Then, when you are ready, slowly count to five, stretch gently, and open your eyes.

You don't have to think about or do anything in particular when you finish this visualization. However, a few couples actually make part or all of their childbirth fantasy a reality. For example, my wife Jan and I had imagined giving birth on top of a mountain. We actually did something similar when our second child, Paul, was born. At the time we were living in a city apartment. Having always wanted to give birth in the country, we rented a home on a hill in central Vermont. There we enjoyed a beautiful home-away-from-home birth attended by a midwife and physician. To complete the celebration, the physician played Renaissance flute music while we bonded with our child.

Imagining the Birth

During this exercise, you give your inner mind a picture of your goal: laboring smoothly in perfect harmony with nature. It is most effective when someone guides you through it and you imagine many contractions.

Molly Connelly, midwife and director of the New Hampshire Childbirth Education Association, guides her clients through this visualization for a full forty minutes. According to her, it can help the mother greet labor with joy and ride above the most difficult contractions peacefully, with less tension, knowing that sne is the source of the power that brings her baby into the world and into her waiting arms.

Relax completely, body and mind.

Begin with *The Special Place* exercise (pages 29–31).

Acknowledge that this is *your* time now—a special time to be with the child you have created.

Let your mind drift ahead in time to the day your baby will be born.

The day you have waited for has come. You are in labor.

Tell your child that the time has come for you to meet face to face. It is a time for celebration.

Think of your baby. Feel the baby inside you.

Look at your baby in your mind's eye. The head is cushioned against your cervix. The back is curled up. The eyes are closed.

Touch your belly if you want. Caress your child within.

You begin to feel a rush of energy deep within your thighs. It comes up and circles your waist, tightens around your belly, and pushes down.

Acknowledge that you are the source of this power and let it come.

The contractions surge, rise to a crest, and ebb away like waves.

The waves of energy keep coming.

You say yes as each new wave comes. Yes. Yes. Yes.

Each wave of power moves your baby down, down, down.

The baby's head pushes against the ring that is your cervix, opening it wider, wider, wider, like a newly blossoming flower touched by the sun's rays.

The waves keep coming. Wave upon wave.

You begin to perspire. Your breathing becomes faster.

But you are still the source of these waves. You welcome them.

Look at your baby again. Your baby is surrounded by the warmth of the waves. He is coming closer and closer to the light.

Again the wave surges. It circles your abdomen. It tightens. You let it happen.

Again a mighty surge of energy tightens and pushes your baby down, down, down.

Take a deep breath. Relax.

You and your baby are grateful for this surge of power. You welcome it as a friend.

Again it comes, tightening, pushing down, down, down.

Take a breath. Feel it tightening.

Imagine your cervix is opened.

Think about your baby coming out.

Now look at your baby again. See the moist curly hair. Look down.

You feel the baby pushing down, down, down.

You feel the head as it slides down, pushing. Your body is kneading and pushing. Kneading and pushing.

Now drift ahead in time. The waves have ceased.

You are cradling your baby in your arms, warm, moist, beautiful, the child you have made, cradled in your arms.

Tell yourself and your baby: We are grateful for this beautiful birth.

Take a minute or so to enjoy the feeling of your newborn child against your breast.

When you are ready, count slowly to five, stretch

gently and open your eyes.

The Ocean

This visualization, based on an exercise from the book M*ind* over L*abor* is a metaphorical way of picturing labor. It inspires confidence in your ability to cope with childbirth.

Relax completely, body and mind.

Imagine yourself on a beautiful natural beach, warm and comfortable.

Imagine the deep blue or emerald green water.

Watch the waves for a few minutes, surging and ebbing, surging and ebbing.

Now imagine that you are out on the water. You are floating securely on the water's surface, perfectly safe.

Each time a wave surges, feel it lifting you, gently supporting the weight of your entire body, carrying you along.

As the waves surge higher, let your breathing become a little deeper, let your body become a little more relaxed.

If thoughts or fears come into your mind, imagine they are pieces of driftwood carried away by the waves.

Feel the waves surging strong, rising, rising, reaching a crest and ebbing, ebbing, ebbing away.

Imagine that these powerful waves are massaging the baby, preparing him or her for the first breath.

The waves are preparing you to welcome your child.

Now allow the waves to bring you to shore. Imagine that you and your baby are together on the shore, warm, relaxed.

Look at your child. Let thoughts and feelings come as they will.

When you are ready, count slowly to five, gently stretch, and open your eyes.

The Invitation

Like a wedding, birth is a celebration of life. It is an intimate family event to be shared among people who feel comfortable together. Those whom you invite to share your birth—especially your caregiver—have a profound impact on your birth experience. This exercise enlists your inner mind's aid in choosing or evaluating your caregiver, labor support person, and whomever else you plan to invite to attend your birth.

Relax completely, body and mind.

Begin with *The Special Place* exercise (pages 29–31).

Enjoy your special place for a few minutes.

Remind yourself: no one can enter this place without my invitation.

Now invite the person or persons with whom you plan to share your birth to enter your special place: your partner, your family, your children, a friend or friends, a labor support person, and finally your caregiver.

As each person enters your special place, ask yourself: Is this someone with whom I want to share this intimate family event? Will this person contribute to a beautiful birth experience?

Allow thoughts to drift into your mind. Don't try to analyze them at this point. Just let them drift freely.

Now thank those who have come to attend your birth for contributing to a safe, fulfilling experience.

Then, when you are ready, count slowly to five, stretch gently, and open your eyes.

When you have finished *The Invitation*, analyze the thoughts that have surfaced. Discuss your feelings with your mate. Make a decision, if appropriate, and act on it. Don't be afraid to change caregivers if being attended by your present physician or midwife doesn't "feel right" to you. A change of caregiver often makes the difference between a safe, natural birth and a cesarean section.

While doing this exercise, one mother had a clear feeling that she should change physicians. Her insurance coverage paid for the particular health care group with whom she was receiving prenatal care and she had never thought of changing. "But the need to change doctors struck me like a flash," she recalls. "I knew I would never have the wonderful birth I wanted if I continued with the same intervention-minded obstetrician."

This mother lost the benefits of her health insurance, but gained a beautiful birth experience.

Birthplace

Whether you give birth at home, in a childbearing center or in a hospital, the most important thing to consider is safety. You want to be sure that you and your baby have the best possible care. At the same time, you, your mate, and your child deserve to have birth take place in an atmosphere suffused with love and peace, and where you—not the attendants around you—are the center of the childbearing drama. This is true even if you have complications.

Bear in mind that birth is the beginning of a family. It is therefore one of the most significant social events in the lives of a couple. In the *Birthplace* exercise, your inner self helps you choose or evaluate your birthing environment with these ideas in mind.

Relax deeply, body and mind.

Begin with *The Radiant Light* exercise (pages 31–32).

Now drift ahead in time.

Imagine that you are in labor.

Picture yourself in your birthing place, or in a birthing place that you are considering.

Take a mental tour of the place.

Now ask yourself the following questions:

• Am I the center of my childbearing experience in this place?

• Am I fully in charge?

• Is this the place where I want to begin a new family?

• Do I receive the emotional support I deserve in this place?

Let thoughts, images, and feelings drift into your mind. Don't try to analyze them. Just let them drift freely.

Then, when you are ready, count slowly to five, stretch gently, and open your eyes.

Analyze what you have thought of in the light of common sense. Discuss your feelings with your mate. Explore several birthing environments with the questions from this exercise in mind. It is never too late to choose a birthing place—as long as you aren't in labor.

Chapter Five

Getting in Touch with Your Unborn Child

As the weeks pass, you may find your thoughts and feelings turning more and more to your baby. Who is this tiny being you are preparing to greet? Is the baby a boy or a girl? What does the baby look like? What will his personality be like?

Focusing on the being within, the three visualization exercises in this chapter take you on an inner journey which can help you prepare for birth and parenthood in several ways.

First, tuning into your growing baby can assist you when making appropriate birth plans or making changes in plans you already have. You may begin to think of the baby's experience of birth. This can guide you to evaluate your choice of caregiver and birthing environment with the baby's experience in mind. For example, when considering a birth environment, you may ask yourself: "Is this really the best place to make the transition to life outside the womb?"

Second, centering on your growing child can reduce self-doubt about your ability to give birth normally. Your inner journey reminds you: Your body has created a new human being. It has made the placenta through which your baby receives everything he needs to grow and be healthy. It has created the curly, bluish-white umbilical cord and the amniotic sac, the waters in which your baby floats content and secure. As you acknowledge the miracle your body is working, you begin to think of labor with confidence.

Third, imagining your baby in utero can help you make emotional adjustments to new parenthood. According to psychologist Leni Schwartz, who has taught mental visualization to thousands of expectant parents and health professionals, it can enhance the family relationship before the baby is born. As you do the exercises, you begin to accept your unborn child as part of your unfolding family and to confront your feelings about becoming a parent. Though nothing can prepare you for what it will be like to be a mother or father twenty-four hours a day, seven days a week, this will help you better handle the change in your lives. Thinking about how life will change after the baby is born may also encourage you to take some concrete steps such as learning about breastfeeding and arranging for household help the first few postpartum days.

Fourth, visualization may enhance the preverbal communication between parents and unborn child. Expectant mothers frequently feel they are communicating with their developing offspring in a language beyond words. For example, Katy, a new mother, recalls, "Throughout pregnancy my husband, John, and I would sometimes carry on a dialogue with our baby. I believe that in her own way she understood us and responded with her little kicks. When John called from work, the baby often kicked excitedly as if she too could hear his voice and recognize that it was Daddy."

There is nothing unusual about this. Many parents have similar experiences. The mother's thoughts and feelings influence the baby via hormones, biochemical processes, and perhaps other means as yet unknown to science. In one striking medical study, Michael Lieberman has shown that the baby is affected not only when the mother smokes but even when the mother was shown a cigarette. This may have been the result of a quickened maternal heart rate or subtle changes in her body chemistry at the sight of a cigarette (Sontag 106).

Strong emotions alter the mother's blood chemistry and, by way of the placenta, the baby's as well. Dr. Lester Sontag of the Fels Research Institute in Yellow Springs, Ohio, has shown that distress in the mother produces a marked increase in fetal activity (Sontag 996-1003). Violent emotional upsets increase fetal activity up to tenfold. Brief maternal stress probably has no long-term effect on the baby, but prolonged stress has been associated with ill health and behavioral difficulties (Stott 781).

By way of contrast, the emotions elicited during visualization may have a calming effect on the baby. According to Thomas Verny, a pioneer in the field of prenatal psychology and author of *The Secret Life of the Unborn Child*, communicating love to your baby within may actually overcome the effects of stress and other negative feelings. Though we cannot be sure, visualization may affect the baby's health in a positive way.

Finally, visualization and dwelling on the love you feel for your child promote prenatal bonding, that is, the parent-infant attachment process.

Inner Bonding

The parent-child relationship begins while the baby is still in the womb. Prenatal bonding—the beginning of parent-child attachment—occurs during pregnancy. Fantasies about the baby, dreams, and such activities as choosing the baby's name and shopping for the layette influence this process. As pregnancy progresses, the mother, and often the father, becomes more emotionally involved with the unborn child.

There is nothing you *need* to do to form a bond with your unborn child. It happens naturally. You don't have to consciously think about fetal development to help him grow. But you *can* enhance the prenatal bond and feel closer to your child by trying the following.

- With a hand on the abdomen, both mother and father can feel the baby's outline. Try to locate and identify arms, legs, back, and head. (Don't be surprised if you can't identify body parts. Most parents have difficulty with this.)

- Talk to your baby. Tell the baby how much you are looking forward to seeing him. Share any ambivalent feelings you have as well.

- Turn your attention inward with the visualization exercises in this chapter. Sylvia Klein Olkin, director of Positive Pregnancy and Parenting Fitness in Baltic, Connecticut, calls this process "inner bonding." According to her, inner bonding can make the transition to parenthood immeasurably smoother and life after the baby is born "much, much easier."

Inner Bonding Visualization

This exercise for both parents is based on an exercise designed by Sylvia Klein Olkin and Frederick Leboyer, French obstetrician and author of *Birth Without Violence*. It is a very simple but wonderfully effective way to promote prenatal bonding. Do it any time during pregnancy.

Relax completely, body and mind.

Quiet your mind by concentrating on your breath flowing in and out.

Allow your breathing to settle down and become a little slower without forcing the breath in any way.

Now imagine your whole being opening up to your unborn child.

Let the love you feel for your child well up within you. Imagine it pouring into your baby.

Now also imagine the bliss, the contentment, the security, and the happiness your baby feels and lives within the womb pouring into you.

Imagine that these wonderful feelings can pass to you through a secret doorway. Open the doorway a bit wider so you can be flooded with these good feelings.

Dwell with your child and with these feelings for a few minutes.

Then, when you are ready, count slowly to five, stretch gently, and open your eyes.

Getting in Touch with Your Unborn Child

This exercise provides a refreshing journey within that can leave you relaxed, revitalized, and feeling more attuned to your baby, as it helps you make emotional adjustments for birth and parenthood.

Both parents can use this visualization. One expectant mother said, after trying *Getting in Touch with Your Unborn Child*, "It gives me a wonderful reassuring feeling, a sense of inner strength and power, and of knowing that my baby and I are making this passage together." John Rehak, host of the popular radio talk show New Age Cleveland, used this exercise when expecting his first child. He remarked, "I have a peaceful sense of staring into my child's eyes, just sharing love between the two of us."

Mother's Version

Relax completely, body and mind.

Focus your mind on your breathing for a minute or so.

Allow your breathing to become a little deeper, a little slower but not forced in any way.

Imagine that you are breathing directly into the womb where your baby is surrounded by crystal clear water in his or her own private world.

Now imagine that your in-breath is a soft, radiant, golden light.

Continue to breathe in the light until it fills your womb and surrounds your baby with a warm, vibrant glow.

Dwell for a minute or so on the soft, glowing, golden light which fills your womb.

Imagine your baby's contentment right now. The womb is a wonderful place to be—secure and warm.

47

Allow the love you feel for your child to well up within you.

Speak to your baby—tell him or her anything you wish—how you are feeling right now, or that you are looking forward to the day when you will hold him or her in your arms.

If you find your attention wandering, mentally repeat the word "baby, baby, baby," and let yourself drift into an even more peaceful, relaxed state, dwelling on your baby.

Enjoy this visualization for a few minutes. When you are ready, count slowly to five, stretch gently, and open your eyes.

Or, if you prefer, remain in your relaxed state and continue on with the next exercise, *Talking with Your Baby* (pages 49–50).

Father's Version

Relax completely, body and mind.

Focus your mind on your breathing for a minute or so.

Allow your breathing to become a little deeper, a little slower, but not forced in any way.

Now imagine that the in-breath is a soft, radiant, golden light.

Continue to breathe in the light until it fills your entire body and radiates from you in all directions.

Imagine that this golden light also surrounds your baby with its soft, vibrant glow and links you with your unborn child. It doesn't matter whether you are in the same room with your mate and your developing baby or a thousand miles away. Right now the soft, golden light that you breathe in connects you with your child.

Now imagine that you are cradling the baby in your arms.

Allow the love that you feel for your child to well up within you. Speak to your baby, tell him or her anything you wish—how you are feeling right now, or sing your baby a lullabye.

If you find your attention wandering, mentally repeat the word "baby, baby, baby," and let yourself drift into an even more peaceful, relaxed state, dwelling on your baby.

Enjoy this visualization for a few minutes, and when you are ready, count slowly to five, stretch gently, and open your eyes.

Or, if you wish, go right on with the next exercise, *Talking with Your Baby* (pages 49–50).

Talking with Your Baby

This exercise is a form of "receptive visualization" in which you ask the baby a specific question and remain open-minded to receive an answer. Receptive visualization is an effective way to tap your inner resources. Some parents believe they are actually communicating with the baby while doing this visualization. Others feel the responses come from their own inner mind.

You may want to ask the baby, "What do you need most right now?" In response, you may think of something missing in your diet, the need for a more understanding caregiver, or simply the need for love.

Another very important question to ask is: "In what kind of place would you like to be born?" Asking this can help you consider possible birth environments from the baby's point of view. In response, you may imagine a specific hospital birthing room or birth environment. You may simply have a mental picture—like an impressionistic painting—of a place full of peace and love.

Whatever question you ask, you may receive an answer in the form of words, a picture in your mind's eye, or simply an impression or "gut feeling."

Or you may receive no answer at all. The exercise is still beneficial. For instance, if you have asked the baby where he would like to be born, you may discover a fresh insight hours, days, or even weeks after doing the exercise.

Relax completely, body and mind

Begin with the exercise *Getting in Touch with Your Unborn Child* (pages 47–49).

Dwell on the image of the soft, radiant, golden light surrounding your baby for a minute or so.

Now ask your baby a question.

Imagine that your baby can answer you in words, in images, with impressions, or by painting a picture in your mind's eye.

If thoughts or impressions enter your mind, take note of them without trying to analyze them just yet.

Then, when you are ready, count slowly to five, gently stretch, and open your eyes.

When you finish this exercise, analyze the answer you have received (if any) in the light of common sense. For example, suppose after asking your baby, "In what kind of place would you like to be born?" you receive a mental impression of an environment where you, your mate, and your child can interact freely without interruption, but the hospital where you plan to give birth does not offer such a setting. Perhaps it would be wise to reconsider your birth plans. Weigh the pros and cons of changing plans and examine all available options before making a final decision.

Though visualization may yield intuitive knowledge, you need to analyze your intuitions carefully to see if they have any practical applications. Think over the idea that has come to mind. Discuss it with your mate. If it makes sense, act on it.

Chapter Six

Creative Visualization During Labor

There is no tool more powerful than creative visualization to reduce the fear and pain of labor and help you enjoy a rewarding birth. According to Dr. Emmett Miller, a world-renowned expert on the subject, using visualization in labor promotes a "higher level of functioning." By helping you relax and surrender to the childbearing experience, visualization may even shorten labor and reduce the chance of fetal distress and other complications. Visualization enables body and mind to work in harmony during the amazing process that brings your child into your waiting arms. This harmony allows your body to do its job in the most efficient way possible.

The Laboring Mind Response

Understanding the psychological changes that take place during labor can help you better appreciate your experience, enable your mate to provide more appropriate support, and help you understand why creative visualization is such an effective tool.

During labor the mother experiences a profound alteration of consciousness. She gradually progresses from her ordinary rational state of mind to a more primal, intuitive state. It is as if the contractions that open the cervix were also opening the door on an instinctive part of herself. This normal psychological response to labor is the *laboring mind response*.

The *laboring mind response* reveals itself in the following mind/body changes:

- *Greater right brain hemisphere orientation.* The focus of the laboring mother's energy seems to shift from the left hemisphere (the rational, logical mind) to the right (instinctive self).

- *Altered perceptions.* The laboring mother's perception of space and time is distorted. Her concentration narrows. She focuses inward. Her contractions and her mate become her world.

- *Heightened emotional sensitivity.* The laboring mother becomes highly sensitive, vulnerable. She is utterly dependent on her mate or those surrounding her.

- *Distinctly sexual behavior.* The laboring mother may moan, sigh, and groan very much like the woman nearing sexual climax. She becomes intensely emotional, and near the time of birth she often wears an ecstatic expression like the woman on the edge of orgasm.

- *Lower inhibitions.* The mother often becomes less concerned about the opinions of those around her, about who sees her unclothed body or hears the primal sounds she makes.

- *Increased openness to suggestion.* The critical remarks of others, tension and disturbance in her birthing environment all affect her deeply and in turn affect the physiology of her labor, often causing longer, more difficult contractions. Likewise, the positive suggestions of creative visualization can bring about a more efficient labor.

It is essential to realize that the laboring mother's uninhibited behavior and the sensual sounds she makes are *normal* and something to be encouraged. They indicate that she is in the ideal state of mind to labor in harmony with nature.

Like lovemaking, labor is a primal function which works best when the analytical mind (the left hemisphere) is set aside and the mother surrenders body and mind to her experience.

Using visualization helps her to do just that.

Instructions for Using Creative Visualization During Labor

Anyone can use visualization to better cope with labor.

The method is most effective if you have practiced it during pregnancy. However, you can still use the exercises in this chapter even if you don't know anything about visualization and are picking up this book for the first time while you are in labor.

Marian Tompson, co-founder of La Leche League International, did just that. She read the book, M*ind over La*bor (which includes visualization exercises) on the very day her daughter, Alison, went into hard labor. She brought the book with her to her daughter's home. When she arrived, Marian found that Alison was having a difficult time. The breathing exercises she had been taught in childbirth class were not helping her relax. Marian suggested she try one of the visualization exercises in the book just to see if it might help. Within a short while, Alison was able to relax and her labor began progressing quickly.

The following guidelines will help you use visualization during labor.

- Read through the exercises in this chapter (both you and your mate).

- Choose those that most appeal to you.

- Do them whenever you feel the need during labor. You

may want to use visualization during some contractions and just relax and breathe rhythmically during others.

• Use any of the images in this chapter at any time during labor.

• During late labor, when there is often little time to rest between contractions, many women find short, simple, visualization such as *The Blossoming Flower*, *The Radiant Breath*, and *Ocean Waves*, most effective. However, if you prefer, you can use any of the others in late labor.

• Use the same visualization over and over with each contraction if you want. Or, if you prefer, vary the images.

• You can do the visualization exercises on your own as your mate or another person gives you other forms of labor support. Or your mate can guide you through the exercises.

Instructions for Guiding a Laboring Woman Through Visualization Exercises

This section is addressed to the father—or to whoever is supporting the laboring mother and guiding her through the visualization exercises.

Ideally you should prepare with the mother in advance for labor. Learn about childbirth during her pregnancy.

Read "The Laboring Mind Response" in this chapter to help you better understand the mother's psychological state during labor.

Learn basic techniques you can use, in addition to creative visualization to reduce the mother's fear and pain. The book, *Sharing Birth: A Father's Guide to Giving Support During Labor*, shows you step by step how to best help the mother through the stages of labor. (See "Recommended Reading.")

To help the mother use creative visualization:

- First read through whatever exercises she plans to use and become familiar with them. It is best to do this in advance of labor, if possible.

- Guide the mother through the exercise in a soft voice. Pause between each step, giving her plenty of time to complete that step before going on to the next.

- If doing a long exercise, such as *The Rainbow* (pages 58–59), you can read the exercise aloud. Otherwise, try to remember the details so you do not have to hold this book while guiding the mother through the exercise.

- As you guide her through the exercise, remember that you are communicating with her "laboring mind," not her ordinary waking consciousness. The "laboring mind" responds to simple images, simple statements. Though it may seem boring to you, you can repeat the same images or positive statements over and over again.

- Remain close physically, provided she feels comfortable with physical contact. (Some women become annoyed at being touched, particularly during late labor.)

- Caress her. Stroke her hair, her arms, her legs, whatever she finds comfortable.

- Share her experience. Get right on the bed with her if she is laboring there. Walk with her if she is up walking. Help her bathe or shower. The bathtub or shower is a great place to use creative visualization.

- It's important to remember that the mother needs to feel secure and protected. That's why your presence is so vital. Shield her from outside disturbances. Let her know it's all right to do her own thing.

- Let her know by your words and actions that her uninhibited behavior is normal. Do *not* discourage her from moaning, groaning, sighing, or vocalizing in any way she pleases. This helps her surrender to labor and actually helps labor progress.

- Since the laboring mother is so open to suggestion, your attitude can make a world of difference. Encourage her. Praise her. Express positive feelings. (This is easier if you have a positive attitude about childbirth yourself.)

- Trust her to labor in the best possible way, even if she seems afraid. Let her know that you believe in her strength and power to give birth.

Visualization Exercise for Labor

The exercises in this chapter are in a slightly different format than the visualization for pregnancy. First, they omit the introductory relaxation exercise, because during labor you'll want to get right into the visualization. Second, they omit the final step, "Count slowly to five, stretch gently, and open your eyes," because you may want to continue using visualization exercises one after the other throughout labor.

The Special Place

Imagining yourself in a wholly comfortable and peaceful environment enables you to feel more secure and relaxed during labor. You can do this exercise at any time during your labor. It is particularly effective if, in the event of labor complications, you must give birth in a highly technical hospital setting.

There are two ways to do this exercise.

1. The first version is for those who have practiced *The Special Place* as described in Chapter 4 (pages 29–31). If you have practiced this exercise during pregnancy, you have probably come to associate your *special place* with inner peace and relaxation.

Imagine yourself in your *special place,* your personal inner sanctuary. Let the details of this setting unfold before your mind's eye.

Either recall the details of this inner sanctuary yourself, or if your mate or another person is familiar with your *special place,* he can recall the details for you in a soft voice, guiding you through the visualization.

2. You can use this second version whether or not you have practiced *The Special Place* during pregnancy.

Imagine yourself in any relaxing place: any place at all, real or imaginary, that makes you feel serene, comfortable, and in touch with your inner strength.

Here are some possibilities:

- a room in your home where no one can disturb you

- a comfortable chair by a cozy fireplace

- on the sand of a beach feeling the warm sun bathing you in its soft, soothing colors.

- near a gentle waterfall

- lying on a mossy carpet near a bubbling brook

- leaning against a great ancient tree absorbing its power, its wisdom

- beneath a beautiful rainbow, which is bathing you in its soft, soothing colors.

Whatever place you choose, use all of your senses—sight, sound, smell, touch, taste—to put yourself in this very special environment. Let the details of your visualization unfold gently before your mind's eye.

The Rainbow

This exercise is wonderfully relaxing. It is very effective if someone guides you through it. However, you can do this exercise quite well without a guide by picturing the colors of the rainbow in your mind's eye.

Imagine that you are lying beneath a beautiful, magical rainbow.

See the rainbow arching over you in the sky.

You are at the rainbow's end.

Feel the rainbow pouring over you, into you, washing through you with its soft, soothing colors.

Give yourself to the rainbow.

Take a deep breath in. Let it out.

As you breathe out, let your tension melt away, dissolving in the rainbow all around you.

Let the rainbow take you on a wondrous journey.

Now, imagine the color red. Breathe in red. Breathe out red. Let everything be red. Red surrounds you with its warmth. You are bathed in the warm rays of red.

Now breathe in the color orange. Breathe out orange. See yourself surrounded by orange, secure in the bright warmth of orange.

As you continue to breathe in and out, let the orange shade to yellow. Sunny yellow sweeps over you, surrounding you with yellow, bathing you in bright yellow energy.

Now, let green flow through you as you breathe in and out. Green surrounds you, washes over you and through you, refreshing and spring-like.

Breathing in and out, imagine the green shading ever so gently to blue. Breathe in blue. Breathe out blue. Let blue wash over you in serene blue waves. You are surrounded by blue, bathed in cool blue.

Now, let the blue fade to indigo. Breathe in indigo. Breathe out indigo. Deep relaxing indigo surrounds you and bathes you in its soothing rays.

Now, let the indigo shade to violet. Breathe in violet. Breathe out violet. Serene, calming violet surrounds you and bathes you.

Relax into the violet. Let yourself go.

Allow yourself to sink gently, comfortably into deep violet, feeling more and more serene. Now, breathe in golden white light. Let the brilliant golden white light grow and grow until everything is golden light.

Breathe in the golden light. Let it surround you. You are bathed in a golden aura of light. Feel the golden light relax and revitalize you.

The Blossoming Flower

An opening flower is the perfect symbol for both the opening cervix and widening vagina. No image better captures the qualities of warmth, beauty, softness, moisture, fragrance, and opening.

This very simple, lovely exercise is the most popular for labor and one of the most effective. Use it any time during your labor, with or between contractions.

Imagine a flower in your mind's eye.

Choose any flower you want—a rose, a lily, a tulip— any flower at all as long as it is beautiful.

Now, imagine the flower opening petal by petal, opening, opening, opening, until it is fully open.

Add as many details as you want to this visualization, whatever most helps you enjoy it: the shape of the petals, their delicate or bold shading, dewdrops on the flower, fragrance, perhaps the sound of birdsong in the distance, or sunshine dancing over the flower, coaxing it to open.

Variations

1. Imagine yourself in a garden surrounded by *hundreds* of beautiful flowers. Take a mental journey in the garden and choose the most beautiful flower of all. Observe the flower blossoming, petal by petal. Add as many details as you like.

2. During contractions you can imagine any kind of circle growing wider and wider. Pat Jones, certified nurse midwife in Houston, sometimes suggests that her clients imagine an ever-widening doughnut hole. Many have found this effective.

The Waterfall

Many women find this exercise effective for reducing tension in the midst of hard labor. It centers the mind on one of the most inspiring of all images: a waterfall, symbolizing nature's power to flow ceaselessly without effort or strain.

Imagine that you are before a beautiful waterfall.

Let the details of this image surround you.

See the crystal-clear water flowing, flowing.

Hear the sound of the waterfall, a gentle, relaxing sound.

Feel the fine spray of the water on your skin, cool and refreshing.

Taste the pure water.

Smell the fragrant air that surrounds this perfect scene.

Now, with each breath you let out, give your tension to the waterfall.

Feel your tension flowing away as you become more and more relaxed, more and more aware of your inner strength.

Tell yourself that you are just like the waterfall, able to flow with your labor effortlessly, without stress.

The Radiant Breath

Rhythmic breathing and creative visualization join hands in this exercise. This healing visualization, based on *Radiant Light* in Chapter 4, puts you in touch with your inner strength, your "birth energy," and helps to relieve tension and discomfort.

Use it any time during labor when you are feeling stress or discomfort.

Take a deep breath in. Let it out.

Now, imagine that with each breath you take in you are breathing in a soft, golden, radiant light.

Imagine that you are breathing this light into your womb, where it surrounds your baby with health-giving energy.

As you continue to breathe this radiant light, imagine that it swells to fill your entire body, your whole being.

Let the radiant light expand and grow until it radiates out from you in all directions, surrounding you with a beautiful golden aura or halo.

Direct the light to any part of your body that feels tense or uncomfortable.

And imagine the tension or discomfort being massaged away by a million fingers of radiant light.

Imagining the Birth

Many laboring mothers find it helpful to focus their mind on the dilating cervix and the baby descending down the birth canal. This realistic visualization can help mind and body work in cooperation.

Sometimes during labor the mother becomes so caught up in the strength of her contractions and the hard, hard work that it is easy to lose sight of everything—even the baby. This exercise helps you welcome the powerful contractions—realizing that they are bringing your baby closer and closer to your waiting arms.

With each contraction, visualize the soft and stretchable cervix opening wider and wider.

Imagine your baby sliding easily down the birth canal, little by little.

Each powerful contraction massages your child, preparing your baby for his or her first breath.

Now imagine your baby sliding out between your legs, coming headfirst into the world and your waiting arms.

As you imagine your cervix dilating and the baby moving down the birth canal, you may want to think of a turtleneck sweater coming over the baby's head. This is a very apt metaphor for the stretching cervix.

Ocean Waves

You can use this relaxing exercise during contractions to help you better flow with your labor and take your mind off the discomfort.

Imagine yourself lying in the ocean, you are taking a wonderful journey.

You are perfectly secure, perfectly safe, cushioned in the water.

Feel a wave lifting you, carrying you along with its majestic strength.

Imagine that each wave is bringing you closer and closer to the shore of a place where you really want to be.

Relax on the wave, relax as completely as you can.

There is nothing you have to do to help the waves. Just be there, floating along with them.

Variations

You can add images to this exercise, repeating it over and over. A longer version can be effective during long contractions, especially if someone guides you through the exercise.

Here are some possibilities:

- Imagine that the pain in your uterus is a wave. Turn your pain into a wave in your mind's eye. It massages your baby, preparing him or her for that first breath as it washes over you, through you.

- Imagine that the waves are warm. Feel the warmth of the waves supporting you, massaging you, massaging you with their warmth.

- Imagine yourself reaching the shore. There, visualize yourself taking your baby in your arms—holding him or her close to your breasts—looking in your baby's eyes, loving your baby.

Enhancing Creative Visualization During Labor

Just as you can use affirmations to enhance visualization exercises during pregnancy, there are also several ways to enhance your visualizations during labor. Common among these are vocalizing, playing music, and chanting. Adjusting your environment, for example by dimming the lights or having comforting items nearby, can also contribute to the effectiveness of creative visualization.

Vocalizing with Creative Visualization

You can try moaning and groaning rhythmically through difficult contractions. For many women this is a very effective coping method especially well suited for late labor. Deep, low moaning or groaning sounds help to dissolve tension and fear and better enable you to surrender to labor.

As one mother put it, "I'm sure I must have sounded like an inebriated cow. But groaning and moaning with tough contractions helped me more than anything else."

Before you're actually in labor, the idea of making such sounds may seem silly or embarrassing. But, the deep resonant sounds of the laboring mother are actually primal, sensual sounds. During labor, your uninhibited, instinctive, "laboring mind" considers vocalizing the natural thing to do.

You may want to let your voice build in volume as the contraction peaks, then fade as the contraction ebbs away. Let the sounds well up from deep within you—shaping themselves in whatever way seems natural at the time.

There are several ways to combine this type of vocalization with visualization. Here are some suggestions:

- Moan or groan deeply with the *out-breath* while doing *The Radiant Breath* exercise (page 61), imagining that the out-breath carries away your tension and pain.

- Moan sensually with the *Ocean Waves* exercise (pages 62-63) as the waves carry you along.

- Groan or moan during the exercise *Imagining the Birth* (pages 36–40) as you imagine the soft, stretchable tissues of the cervix opening more and more.

Your mate may want to groan with you if he is comfortable about it. This can make you feel more at ease and encourage your uninhibited behavior.

Music with Creative Visualization

Music can provide relaxation, diversion, and a focal point for your inner journey with visualization. If you wish, have a tape of beautiful music available to enjoy during labor. Soothing and gentle music is most conducive to creative visualization. Choose something that helps you feel relaxed and allows you to daydream or drift into a reverie.

One mother brought a tape of relaxing harp music to the childbearing center where her baby was born. "During some contractions I practiced gentle rhythmic breathing—deep and slow. During others I centered my mind on one of two mental visualization exercises—*Radiant Breath* throughout the first half of labor and *The Blossoming Flower* closer to the time of birth—everything to the background of the gentle music."

Chanting with Creative Visualization

Since ancient times, people have used rhythmic chanting to bring about a state of deep relaxation and reverie.

You can very effectively combine chanting with creative visualization to help you relax, center your mind on the visualization, and focus away from discomfort. Chanting is especially well-suited to simple visualization exercises such as *The Radiant Breath* (page 61).

Chant any word or phrase you wish. If you meditate regularly and use a *mantra*— that is, a sound repeated silently or aloud while meditating—you can use the same sound during labor.

Or you can use any word with or without meaning. An especially effective word to repeat is "open." Sanskrit words and expressions, such as "Om Mani Padme Hum," are also quite popular in chants.

You can make up your own words or sounds if you want. Or you can use a simple formula or affirmation such as those found in Chapter 4 (pages 27–29) and Chapter 7 (page 69).

Additional Ways to Enhance Creative Visualization

Creative visualization is most effective if you are in a comfortable setting. Dim the lights. To minimize interruptions, your mate can ask people *not* to talk to you during contractions.

Forget the clock. As long as the baby is healthy, it is best to let nature take its course, to allow your body to labor in its own way.

If you must use electronic fetal monitoring, don't get caught up in looking at the machine. This is especially important for the father. Leave reading the machine's tracings to medical experts.

Occasionally the presence of a particular person inhibits labor. Sometimes a friend, a nurse, or caregiver, for example, gives the mother "performance anxiety," especially if this person is watching the clock, expecting you to labor within a certain time. If someone makes you feel uptight, don't be afraid to politely ask that person to leave you alone for a while. Often this is all that is needed to pick up a flagging labor.

Some women who are laboring in a hospital or childbearing center bring a favorite picture or stuffed animal to make the setting a bit more "homey."

One laboring mother and those she invited to her birth wore party hats to remind themselves that this was an occasion to celebrate.

Another woman incorporated details of her *special place* into the hospital birthing room. Her special place was a South Seas island where she and her husband planned to vacation shortly after the baby was born. Among other things she brought to the birthing room were coconut shell drinking cups, a tape of island music, and a bikini (to remind her she would soon be slim again!).

Be creative. Make your birthing environment special in whatever way makes you most comfortable. Remember, giving birth is a celebration. It is *your* very special day.

Welcoming Your Child

After the baby is born, the father may want to cut the cord. If so, let your caregiver know in advance that you plan to do this.

The father's cutting the cord can be a beautiful symbolic gesture—like putting the ring on the bride's finger.

Cordcutting is painless to mother and baby.

The cord will continue pulsing for a while as blood passes from the placenta to the baby. Delay cutting until this pulsing ceases (unless there is a medical reason for doing otherwise).

The caregiver will first prepare the cord, clamping it in two places.

Then, with a pair of scissors, the father cuts between the clamps.

As the cord is cut, you may both want to offer a prayer of thanksgiving for the birth, and for the baby.

Then you may want to utter a prayer of welcome: Welcome, child, into our home.

Chapter Seven

Using Creative Visualization in Special Situations

Childbearing does not always progress as smoothly as nature designed. Complications sometimes arise.

Though visualization cannot guarantee a pregnancy or labor without problems, it can reduce the chance of complications and it can help you cope with problems should they arise.

Cesarean Prevention

In 1985, the U.S. cesarean birth rate was an appalling 22.7 percent. The overwhelming majority of these surgical births are unnecessary and can be prevented. You can increase your chance of a normal vaginal birth by combining the use of visualization with such practical steps as choosing a caregiver and birthing environment with a low cesarean rate.

Your beliefs and attitudes play a major role in shaping your birth experience. During pregnancy, suggestion has a profound impact. Pat Jones, a certified nurse midwife in Houston, and an expert on using creative visualization for a better childbearing experience, observes: "Some well-meaning physicians plant the idea of a cesarean birth in the mother's mind with comments such as, 'Your pelvis is a little small,' or 'Your baby is becoming quite large,' and so forth. They do this so the mother won't be overly disappointed if she does birth surgically."

"I've observed many labors actually stop midstream as a result of one of these suggestions. When labor stops and I encourage the mother to examine possible underlying fears, I often find that she has the idea that her pelvis is too small. Confronting this fear and affirming that she can birth naturally are enough to overcome the problem and get labor progressing again."

Use affirmations during pregnancy to give yourself a positive view of birth and to inspire confidence in your body's ability to birth naturally. Cesarean prevention affirmations might include:

Childbirth is a normal process.

Childbirth is safe.

I am able to birth naturally.

I open for my baby.

My uterus is dependable and strong.

See Chapter 4 for additional affirmations. Use the visualization exercise *Imagining the Birth* in Chapter 4 (pages 36-40). Go through many contractions in your mind. See yourself handling labor smoothly. Imagine the baby being born. Visualize the baby sliding out of the birth canal between your legs (this part of the visualization is very important).

Imagine yourself taking the baby in your arms and expressing gratitude for this wonderful natural birth experience. Use affirmation with the exercise.

Repeat this visualization exercise many times during pregnancy.

If you believe you have an actual physical condition (small pelvis, breech baby, and so forth) which decreases your chance of giving birth vaginally, consult the book *Birth Without Surgery* for specific suggestions (see Recommended Reading). Nine times out of ten, you can still give birth vaginally.

Turning a Breech Baby

If your baby is in a breech position—that is, buttocks or feet presenting first in the birth outlet—birth can be more difficult. It is therefore best to turn the baby prior to your due date. Some physicians and midwives are skilled at doing this by manipulating the baby with hands on the abdomen. However, you may be able to encourage the baby to turn at home.

The following combination of creative visualization and position is very effective for turning a breech baby. Dr. Juliet M. DeSa Souza has recommended this position to hundreds of expectant mothers who have used it with great success. Suzanna May Hilbers, registered physical therapist and teacher trainer for ASPO/ Lamaze, recommends the second of the accompanying exercises.

Do this exercise only with your caregiver's approval.

Lie flat on your back with knees bent, feet flat on the floor, with pillows or cushions under your buttocks so your pelvis is about a foot off the floor.

While in this position, do one of the following visualization exercises:

Imagine the baby floating in fluid, head down and comfortable, resting on a little pillow of crystal clear water.

Imagine children tumbling or doing somersaults, clothes turning in a dryer, or anything else that symbolizes turning.

Most physicians today perform a cesarean section for breech babies, though a few midwives and doctors are skilled with vaginal breech delivery. If your baby does not turn and you want to birth vaginally, see *Birth Without Surgery* for suggestions (see Rec ommended Reading)

Hypertension

Some women develop elevated blood pressure during pregnancy. This is known as gestational hypertension and disappears after giving birth.

Often, increased blood pressure is accompanied by swelling as a result of water retention (though some swelling is normal) and protein in the urine. This condition is known as preeclampsia. No one knows what causes preeclampsia, though some health professionals believe it is the result of poor nutrition.

If you have pregnancy-induced hypertension or preeclampsia, it is essential to be in the care of a good physician or midwife and to follow your caregiver's advice.

Additionally, you can use deep relaxation exercises and creative visualization to try to correct the problem.

Use the *Autogenic Stress Release* exercise in Chapter 3 (pages 21-23).

You can also try the very effective tape, *Down with High Blood Pressure*, by Emmett Miller, M.D. (see Recommended Reading).

Overdue Labor

Only about 5 percent of labors actually begin on their expected due date. It is perfectly normal for labor to begin two weeks earlier or later. As long as the baby is healthy, there is no cause for concern. However, sometimes labor does not begin—even when the baby is fully mature and ready to be born.

The usual in-hospital remedy is induction of labor with Pitocin (an artificial form of the hormone, oxytocin). Unless there is a medical emergency, Pitocin induction should *always* be a last resort to be used *only after* all other means of labor induction have been tried. Pitocin-induced contractions are usually more painful and difficult to manage. In addition, this form of labor induction increases the risk of a cesarean section.

Creative visualization sometimes helps trigger an overdue labor particularly if the delay is due to an emotional conflict, such as fear of childbirth or strong negative feelings about becoming a mother.

To help release possible emotional blocks, try the following:

Do one of the deep mind/body relaxation exercises in Chapter 3.

Then do the *The Special Place* visualization in Chapter 4 (pages 29–31).

While in your special place, ask yourself, Am I ready for my baby to be born?

Let thoughts and feelings drift through your mind freely.

If strong negative feelings surface, it may help to discuss these with your mate and/or a counselor. Confronting and releasing negative feelings is sometimes enough to help you yield to labor.

Another way to examine your feelings and tap your intuition is using the exercise, *Talking with Your Baby*, described in Chapter 5 (pages 49–50). Ask your baby what, if anything, is holding him back.

Other visualization exercises you can try include *Imagining the Birth* in chapter 4 (pages 36–39) and *The Blossoming Flower* in Chapter 4 (pages 59–60).

The following are some additional means to trigger labor. These should be tried *before* considering Pitocin induction. But *check with your caregiver first*. (If your caregiver is unaware of the effectiveness of these remedies, consult another midwife or physician who *fully supports* natural birth.)

- Take a long walk, preferably up and down hills.

- Try eating gas-producing spicy food. For some reason not fully understood, intestinal activity sometimes triggers uterine contractions when the cervix is ripe and you are ready to labor.

72

- Make love vigorously, preferably with orgasm. (Orgasm releases the hormone oxytocin, which may stimulate labor, but does so *only* when the cervix is ripe and the baby is ready to be born.) Avoid intercourse if the bag of waters has been broken.

- Try nipple stimulation, which also releases oxytocin.

- Use castor oil with your caregiver's instructions.

Prolonged Labor

Like every snowflake, every labor is different. Some take place within a few hours—or less—while other labors occur over a period of several days with contractions occurring on and off.

Occasionally the laboring mother "takes a pause," like a hiker stopping to rest on a long mountain walk. Then, when she is ready, labor resumes again.

It is important to realize that a long labor or a pause is perfectly normal provided the baby is healthy.

Some caregivers expect women to complete their labor within a specified time period. This is like expecting someone to achieve orgasm within so many minutes. The very idea of a time limit can inhibit labor's progress. One of the most important things to do, therefore, is to choose a caregiver who has no such restrictions.

As with overdue labor, the usual in-hospital remedy for a prolonged labor is augmentation with Pitocin. Since Pitocin causes more painful and more difficult-to-manage contractions and increases the risk of cesarean surgery, it should be a last-resort measure, to be used only *after* all other remedies have been tried. (See the Overdue Labor section on pages 71–73.)

Creative visualization can sometimes help an overly long labor progress more quickly. Exercises to use include *Imagining the Birth* (pages 36–40), and *The Blossoming Flower* (pages 59–60).

Occasionally, an emotional conflict holds labor up. You can use the same exercises suggested for overdue labor to help release emotional blocks.

Additional remedies for prolonged labor are also the same as those for overdue labor. Avoid intercourse, however, if the bag of waters has broken.

As discussed in Chapter 6, ("Additional Ways to Enhance Creative Visualization," pages 66–67), sometimes a particular person in the birthing environment makes the mother feel tense enough to actually inhibit her labor. If this seems to be the case, feel free to ask this person to leave you alone for a short while. Sometimes this is all that is needed to get labor going again.

Laboring in a Clinical Setting

It is best to choose a peaceful, comfortable birthing environment where you feel that you—not the staff—are the center of the childbearing experience.

However, this is not always possible. For example, the mother with medical complications may be safest giving birth in a hospital with all the latest available technology. On occasion, the mother planning a home or childbearing center birth may have to be transferred at the last minute to the hospital.

Of course, the mother should have the opportunity to use a peaceful birthing room whether or not she has medical problems. However, in some institutions the environment is clinical and impersonal.

Visualization can help you feel more comfortable in a less than ideal birthing environment. The most effective visualization to use is *The Special Place* in Chapter 4 (pages 29–31). Your mate or another person can guide you through this exercise.

In addition to using visualization, your mate should learn everything he can about giving effective labor support. Though always important, labor support takes on a much greater significance in a clinical setting. You might also consider hiring an experienced labor support person.

Recovery from Cesarean Surgery

A cesarean section is occasionally necessary to preserve the health of mother and/or baby. Though one can't minimize the reality of surgery or the loss of a vaginal birth, a necessary cesarean need not be an entirely negative experience.

Creative visualization sometimes helps the healing process.

Visualize the incision site in your mind's eye healing rapidly.

Imagine yourself walking around without discomfort.

Tell yourself you are healing rapidly.

You can also try *The Radiant Breath* in Chapter 6 (page 61) to help you feel relaxed and revitalized.

The scar on the mother's belly is not the only one following a cesarean birth. The book *Birth Without Surgery* suggests that a cesarean section is accompanied by *surgical birth trauma*—a constellation of physical and emotional consequences affecting the entire family.

One of the common consequences of surgical birth is maternal-infant separation, which is one of the major causes of postpartum blues. If you and your baby are separated, try this exercise:

Talk to your baby, either in your imagination or aloud.

Tell your baby how much you missed giving birth to him or her vaginally and how much you missed holding him in your arms during those first minutes after birth.

This healing visualization can help you release your feelings and enhance the parent-infant bond, which sometimes suffers a temporary setback after surgical birth.

Most women are disappointed that they have missed a vaginal birth. Grief is an appropriate reaction, particularly if you believe your cesarean was unnecessary. Allow yourself to grieve. This will help to heal the emotional scars. Most fathers, too, are upset about cesarean surgery. Some blame themselves. They believe they did not provide adequate support.

Talk about your feelings with one another.

Sometimes it helps to remind each other that though cesarean surgery is an unfortunate event, it is still an occasion to celebrate. A child is born.

Don't hesitate to contact a group such as C/SEC, which provides emotional support for cesarean parents as well as practical information about cesarean prevention. (See Resources.)

Using visualization can reduce the chance of complications, including cesarean section, and decrease the need for pain-relief medication. However, sometimes complications arise even in the face of the most well-planned birth and the best of prenatal care. In such a case, visualization can help you cope and enable you to experience the best possible birth under the circumstances.

List of
Exercises
in this Book

Relaxation Exercises

Visualizations for Pregnancy

Visualizations to Prepare for Parenthood

Visualizations for Labor

Visualizations for Special Situations

Works Cited

Benson, Herbert, *Your Maximum Mind*, New York, New York Times Books, 1987.

Gawain, Shakti, *Creative Visualization*, Mill Valley, California: Whatever Publishing, 1978.

Sontag, Lester W., "Prenatal Determinants of Postnatal Behavior," in *Fetal Growth and Development*, Waisman and Kerr, eds. New York: McGraw-Hill, 1970.

Sontag, Lester W., "The Significance of Fetal Environmental Differences," *American Journal of Obstetrics and Gynecology*, vol 42, 1941. pp 996-1003.

Stott, D.H., "Follow-up Study from Birth and the Effects of Prenatal Stress, *Developmental Medicine in Neurology*, vol 15, 1973.

Recommended Reading

Childbirth Preparation

Mind over Labor by Carl Jones. Viking/Penguin, 1986. A complete guide to preparing for childbirth and reducing the fear and pain of labor based on the mind's influence on birth.

David, We're Pregnant by Lynn Johnston. Meadowbrook and Simon & Schuster, 1975. Cartoons by the creator of the "For Better or For Worse" comic strips depict the lighter side of childbirth.

Positive Pregnancy Fitness by Sylvia Klein Olkin. Avery Publishing Group, 1987. A guide to a more comfortable pregnancy and easier birth through exercise and relaxation.

Childbirth Without Fear by Grantly Dick-Reid, MD. Harper, 1984. A beautiful and inspiring classic about natural childbirth.

A Good Birth and a Safe Birth by Diana Korte and Roberta Scaer. Bantam, 1984.

Cesarean Birth and Prevention

Birth Without Surgery by Carl Jones. Dodd, Mead & Co., 1987. A complete step-by-step guide to reducing the chance of cesarean surgery.

Silent Knife—Cesarean Prevention and Vaginal Birth after Cesarean by Nancy Wainer Cohen and Lois J. Estner. Bergin and Gawley Inc., 1983.

Labor Support

The Birth Partner's Handbook by Carl Jones with Jan Jones. Meadowbrook, 1989. This handbook gives full instructions for fathers, friends, and relatives who are helping a mother in labor.

The Labor Support Guide—For Fathers, Family and Friends (pamphlet) by Carl Jones, Henci Goer, and Penny Simkin. (Available from Pennypress, Inc., 1100 23rd Avenue East, Seattle, WA 98112.) Instructions for helping the laboring mother. An eight-page pamphlet for easy reference during labor.

Sharing Birth: A Father's Guide to Giving Support During Labor by Carl Jones. William Morrow, 1985. A concise handbook which shows the father, or anyone planning to help a woman through labor, how to reduce the fear and pain of childbirth step by step through the stages and phases of labor.

For Fathers

The Birth of a Father by Martin Greenbery, M.D. Avon, 1988. A practical guide to pregnancy, birth and beyond.

The New Father: Survival Guide by Larry Snydal and Carl Jones. Franklin Watts, Inc., 1987. A light, humorous practical guide, this book shows the new dad how to best help his mate and meet his own needs through the life-transforming first weeks of parenthood.

The Postpartum Period

After the Baby is Born by Carl Jones. Dodd, Mead & Co., 1986. America's most widely recommended postpartum guide, this complete handbook for new parents discusses the physical and emotional changes that follow having a baby and shows how to relieve the new mother's discomforts, regain the pre-pregnant shape in the shortest possible time, and safely resume the sexual relationship.

Baby and Child Medical Care by Terril H. Hart, MD, ed. Meadowbrook and Simon & Schuster, 1982. A complete, up-to-date, easy-to-use, first aid book for parents.

Feed Me I'm Yours by Vicki Lansky. Meadowbrook and Simon & Schuster, 1986. Baby food made easy, delicious, nutritious and fun things to cook up for your kids.

First Year Baby Care Paula Kelly, MD, ed. Meadowbrook and Simon & Schuster, 1983. An illustrated, step-by-step baby care guide for new parents.

The Well Baby Book by Mike Samuels, MD. and Nancy Samuels. Summit Books, 1979. A comprehensive, up-to-date guide to holistic health care through the first year of life.

Breastfeeding

Breastfeeding Your Baby: A Complete Guide for the Nursing Family by Carl Jones and Jan Jones. Dodd, Mead, 1988. Fully involving the father, this handbook provides practical information about preparing to breastfeed, nursing from birth to weaning, relieving the common breastfeeding discomforts, and using mental imagery to enhance successful nursing.

Successful Breastfeeding by Nancy Dana and Anne Price. Meadowbrook and Simon & Schuster, 1985. A practical guide for nursing mothers.

The Working Woman's Guide to Breastfeeding by Nancy Dana and Anne Price. Meadowbrook and Simon & Schuster, 1987. A book that addresses and provides solutions for working mothers wishing to breastfeed. Complete and comprehensive.

Resources

Breastfeeding

La Leche League International, 9616 Minneapolis Avenue, Franklin Park, Illinois 60131. (312)455-7730. Provides information and support about breastfeeding without charge. LLLI has thousands of nursing counselors, or leaders, throughout the country to answer questions. If you cannot find a listing in your local telephone directory, call the main office for a reference.

Cesarean Birth

C/Sec, Inc. 22 Forest Road, Framingham, MA 01701. (617)877-8266. Provides information on cesarean birth prevention and offers emotional support to cesarean families.

Cassette Tapes

Letting Go of Stress by Emmett Miller, M.D. Very effective exercises for deep relaxation.

Down with High Blood Pressure by Emmett Miller, M.D. Imagery exercises to relax away tension and lower high blood pressure.

Rainbow Butterfly by Emmett Miller, M.D. Beautiful imagery exercises to relax deeply and experience inner serenity and creativity.

Three tapes just listed are available from Source, P.O. Box W, Dept. L, Stanford, CA 94305. (415) 328-7171.

Relax and Enjoy Your Baby Within by Sylvia Klein Olkin Imagery for relaxation, as well as communicating with and loving your child within. Available for Be Healthy, Inc., 5 Saltrock Road, Baltic, CT 06330 1-800-433-5523.

Exercises for Baby & Me
by Susan L. Regnier
The YMCA's prenatal, postpartum and infant exercise book. A physiologically and medically approved program. Now with more photographs, step-by-step instructions and exercises than any other book. **$9.95**
Order #1099

First-Year Baby Care
by Paula Kelly, M.D.
This handbook covers the first twelve months of life — when parents need help most! The step-by-step photos and illustrations make the up-to-date, authoritative information easy to use. This book covers bathing, diapering, feeding, first aid, child-proofing and more. **$6.95**
Order #1159

Successful Breastfeeding
by Nancy Dana and Anne Price
This the most practical illustrated guide for nursing mothers. It tells how to overcome the most common problems and complications mothers meet in breastfeeding. **$9.95**
Order #1199

Pregnancy, Childbirth and the Newborn
by Simkin, Whalley, and Keppler
The Childbirth Education Association of Seattle's illustrated guide to pregnancy and childbirth, nutrition, health, exercise, labor and birth, breastfeeding and new baby care. The most widely used prenatal training text in America. **$10.95**
Order #1169

The Best Baby Shower Book
by Courtney Cooke
Who says baby showers have to be dull? Finally, a contemporary guide for planning baby showers that's chock-full of helpful hints, recipes, decorating ideas and activities that are fun without being juvenile. **$4.95**
Order #1239

Getting Organized for Your New Baby
by Maureen Bard
The fastest way to get organized for pregnancy, childbirth and new baby care. Busy expectant parents will love the checklists, forms schedules, charts and hints because they make getting ready so much easier. **$4.95**
Order #1229

Order Form

Qty	Title	Author	Order No.	Unit Cost	Total
	Baby & Child Medical Care	Hart, T.	1159	$6.95	
	Best Baby Name Book	Lansky, B.	1029	$4.95	
	Best Baby Shower Book	Cooke, C.	1239	$4.95	
	Birth Partner's Handbook	Jones, C.	1309	$5.95	
	David, We're Pregnant!	Johnston, L.	1049	$4.95	
	Discipline Without Shouting or Spanking	Wyckoff/Unell	1079	$5.95	
	Exercises for Baby & Me	Regnier, S.	1099	$9.95	
	First-Year Baby Care	Kelly, P.	1119	$6.95	
	Getting Organized for Your New Baby	Bard, M.	1229	$4.95	
	Letters from a Pregnant Coward	Armor, J.	1289	$6.95	
	Pregnancy, Childbirth, and the Newborn	Simkin/Whalley/Keppler	1169	$10.95	
	Practical Parenting Tips	Lansky, V.	1179	$6.95	
	Successful Breastfeeding	Price/Dana	1199	$9.95	
	Visualizations for an Easier Childbirth	Jones, C.	1330	$4.95	
	Working Woman's Guide to Breastfeeding	Price/Dana	1259	$6.95	

				Subtotal	
Meadowbrook Press			Shipping and Handling (see below)	
			MN residents add 6% sales tax	
			Total	

YES, please send me the books indicated above. Add $1.25 shipping and handling for the first book and $.50 for each additional book. Add $2.00 to total for books shipped to Canada. Overseas postage will be billed. Allow up to 4 weeks for delivery. Send check or money order payable to Meadowbrook Press. No cash or C.O.D.'s please. Quantity discounts available upon request.

Send book(s) to:
Name_____

Address_____

City_____ State_____ Zip_____

☐ Check enclosed for $_____, payable to Meadowbrook Press

☐ Charge to my credit card (for purchases of $10.00 or more only)

☐ Phone Orders call: (800) 338-2232 (for purchases of $10.00 or more only)

Account #_____ ☐ Visa ☐ MasterCard

Signature_____ Exp. date_____

Meadowbrook Press, 18318 Minnetonka Boulevard, Deephaven, MN 55391 (612) 473-5400
Toll free (800) 338-2232